THE SŪTRAS ON
THE 5-FOLD ACT
OF DIVINE CONSCIOUSNESS

2023 Revised Edition – Includes the Verses On Surrender

Other Books By This Author

VIBRATION OF DIVINE CONSCIOUSNESS
A Spiritual Autobiography
By Sadguru Kedarji

ISBN: 979-8-218-13365-8
The Bhakta School of Transformation, Inc.

THE VERSES ON WITNESS CONSCIOUSNESS
By Sadguru Kedarji

ISBN: 978-0-578-38070-4
The Bhakta School of Transformation, Inc.

THE ABODE OF GRACE
BHAGAWAN NITYANANDA OF GANESHPURI
By Sadguru Kedarji

ISBN: 979-8-218-18009-6
The Bhakta School of Transformation, Inc.

THE SŪTRAS ON
THE 5-FOLD ACT
OF DIVINE CONSCIOUSNESS

2023 Edition – Includes The Verses On Surrender

Sadguru Kedarji

The Bhakta School of Transformation, Inc.
Youngstown, OH

The Sūtras On The 5-Fold Act of Divine Consciousness

2023 Edition – Includes The Verses On Surrender

Copyright © 2023 by Sadguru Kedarji

Copies of this book may be ordered through booksellers everywhere or by contacting:

Nityananda Shaktipat Yoga
www.NityanandaShaktipatYoga.org
330-623-7388 Ext. 10

ISBN-979-8-218-19915-9

Printed in the United States of America

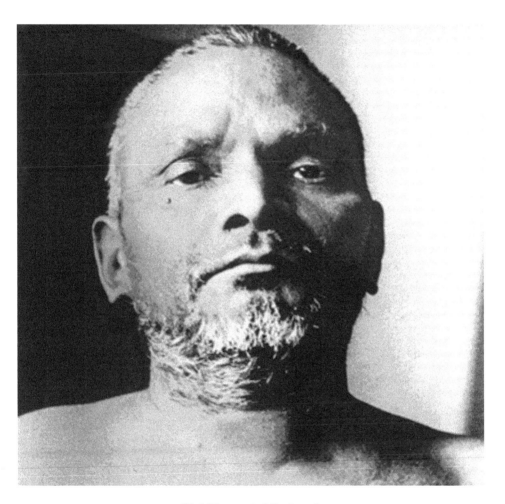

Shri Bhagawān Nityānanda
The Master of Sadguru Kedarji's Lineage

Contents

Foreword

The Sūtras On The 5-Fold Act of Divine Consciousness form a unique work of divine inspiration. These Sūtras can confer Shiva's Bliss on every reader. One of the special qualities of this matchless work is that it can bestow spiritual happiness, both momentarily and continuously. The more one reads and meditates on it, the more one realizes its spiritual depth and its perennial inspiration.

Professor K. Śivananda Kamath
Hosdurg, Kanhangad
Kerala, India

Simple Pronunciation Table

Below we have selected common transliteration from Sanskrit vowels and consonants and given you an English word that will aide you in its proper pronunciation. Please see the glossary for further information.

a	as in cup.
ā	as in father.
i	as in fill or lily.
ī	as in seen.
u	as in full.
ū	as in rude.
ṛi	as in written.
ṛī	as in marine.
e	as in cave.
c	as in church.
ai	as in aisle.
o	as in stone.
au	as in house.
ś	as in sure.
ṣ	as in shun or bush
s	as in saint.
d	as in the th in gather.

Acknowledgements

I dedicate this book to and offer it at the lotus feet of my lineage of Shaktipat Sadgurus, the Self-realized Love Beings, embodied in my 3 in 1, Shri Gurudev Muktananda Paramahamsa, Sri Gurudev Bhagawān Nityānanda and Lord Shiva. I owe my existence to Bhagawān Nityānanda and his disciple, Paramahamsa Muktānanda by whose Grace I received Śaktipat and the Blessings and instruction of Sri Gurudev. It is by the Grace of Gurudev, that I have this golden life filled with the experience of the Absolute.

I offer my thanks to the Primordial Guru of all, the first Sadguru and Supreme Being, my sweet *Lord Śiva* and his *Mahā Spanda Śakti*. It is He, the ashen-covered Blue Being, who gave me my final mantra, ushered in the final realization of my spiritual practice and gave me the command to teach in this way. *It is by His command that I write this book.* To Him be the glory.

My never ending gratitude also goes to Sri Abhinavaguptacharya, Sri Swami Lakshmanjoo and Jñāneshwar Mahāraj who have blessed me with the vision of their inner darshan and guided and inspired me to complete this work.

I also wish to thank Professor K. Śivananda Kamath, one of the elder disciples and servants of Bhagawān Nityānanda, for taking the time to review this book and for sharing his experience of it. He was one of the few remaining "torch bearers" of Sri Nityānanda Bhagawān's legacy and that of Tulsi Amma (one of Nityānanda Baba's greatest disciples also), having served Bhagawān Nityananda in many ways and also at His mother ashram in Kanhangad.

Introduction

The Paradise of Joy

kahain Kabīr vicar ke

*Kabīr ponders and says: "He who has neither
caste nor country, who is formless and without
quality, fills all space." The Creator brought into
being this Paradise of Joy: and from the word Om
the Creation sprang. The earth is His joy; His joy
is the sky;*

*His joy is the flashing of the sun and the moon;
His joy is the beginning, the middle, and the end;
His joy is eyes, darkness, and light.
Oceans and waves are His joy: His joy the Sarāswatī,
the Jumna and the Ganges.*

*The Guru is One: and life and death, union and
separation, are all His plays of joy!
His play the land and water, the whole universe!
His play the earth and the sky!
In play is the Creation spread out, in play it is established.*

*The whole world, says Kabīr, rests in His play,
yet still the Player remains unknown.*

*The poet saint Kabīr
Songs of Kabīr, III. 76.*

I'm going to ask you to keep an open mind while your read this book. **I'm also going to ask you to set your ego aside completely.** Now I'm going to ask you to do one more thing. *Imagine this:*

Imagine that you are the *author of the Universe.* You've just written the first scene in a play entitled MY MANIFESTATION. So far, so good. There are beautiful flowers, plants, trees, land, lakes, creepers of all kinds and oceans in this scene. You've also included a beautiful sky that stretches as far as the eye can see.

The scene also includes air, water, fire, and ether. Everything in this scene, so far, contains an original magnificence and pure beauty that is yours, untainted.

Now you decide to write the second scene. But you realize that you have no characters yet. As you start to ponder the characters you want in this play of yours, you realize that there are so many you like that you can't possibly include just a few. You also decide that you want to have a go at playing each of your characters yourself. So now you've cast yourself in your own play, just for the fun of it.

As you start to play the various roles, you realize how much fun it would be if, rather than writing the whole play before presenting it, you just improvised each scene as you go along. And so, you set out on a magnificent journey, in a play of your own creation that has no real beginning and no end. Now the stage is set for a Supreme Adventure in a Paradise of Joy.

Imagine this as you read these pages.

> *The Highest Lord ever brings about the five-fold act.*
> *He is, in fact, the very Grace itself, being always equipped*
> *with His Supreme Divine Energy (Śakti) whose very nature is*
> *Grace.*
>
> Sri Abhinavagupta
> Parātrīśikā Vivaraṇa

Introduction to The 5-Fold Act of Divine Consciousness

Even in this condition (of the empirical self), he (the individual) does the five kṛtyas (deeds) like Him (like Śiva).

Pratyabhijñāhṛdayam 10

It is through the constant, unimpeded awareness **of The 5-Fold Act of Divine Consciousness,** the 5 Kṛtyas, that one realizes the Self. *Śiva* performs this 5-Fold Act unceasingly. The individual soul also performs this same 5 Fold-Act in a limited way, from birth to death. The 5-Fold Act of Divine Consciousness is: Manifestation, Sustenance (maintenance), Withdrawal (dissolution), Concealment and Grace.

THE TWO ASPECTS OF GOD

A person truly understands God only when he knows both of His aspects. Otherwise, his knowledge is incomplete.

Paramahamsa Muktānanda

Awareness of The 5-Fold Act of Divine Consciousness also brings about another awareness; that of the two aspects of Śakti. Actually, the Śaiva Āgamas state that there are three aspects, the third being the subtle aspect. However, the subtle is contained in each of the other two which is why the Siddhas state it as two.

Every activity (energy) can be seen as having two aspects. **The first is the transcendental (limitless) aspect which represents the outlook of Śiva-Śakti, the experience of the Divine. The second is the immanent (limited) aspect that is the outlook of the Jīva (unenlightened soul).** You can also think of transcendental as the *expanded* form and immanent as the *contracted* form of the same one energy of activity (Vimarśa).

For example, one can see an object, like a jar, as a mere object. This is the *immanent* (limited) aspect of that perception. Or one can experience that same jar as pure Spanda Śakti, as pure Divine

Consciousness Energy, a reflection of Lord Śiva himself. This is the *transcendental* (limitless) aspect of that same perception.

You can think of it in this way: **You can become aware of The 5 Kṛtyas from the limited perspective of the individual bound soul or from the limitless perspective of Śiva.** Your awareness of this 5-Fold Act will determine your state of mind and your ability to experience Samādhi.

Lokānandaḥ Samādhisukham

The delight that the yogi feels in abiding in his nature as the knower in respect of both the subject and the object in the world, is his delight of samādhi.

Śiva Sutras 1:18

So, the Joy of this world is the Ecstasy of Samādhi. What is Samādhi? It has long been thought that Samādhi is the state of pure Bliss experienced in Meditation by those who are very advanced in their practice. Although necessary as a "stepping stone" to Liberation, this experience is not true Samādhi.

Really, *Samādhi* is the state of *Purnaham Vimarśa*, the state in which one experiences God in everything and in everyone, everywhere. It is the constant awareness that it is Śiva alone, Divine Consciousness, that exists everywhere inside and out. The individual subject and object are only reflections of the inner knower. This is the highest state of consciousness, known as *Turyātīta* or *Śiva Vyapti*.

In this state, even the distinction between transcendental and immanent dissolves. For one who is in this state, the Universe does not exist. For such a person, the entire Cosmos is a *Play of Divine Consciousness* emanating from inside one's own Self.

This state comes about through practicing the awareness of The 5-Fold Act of Divine Consciousness and the two aspects of Śiva. The practice of this awareness is supported and made possible through Śaktipat and Meditation. Again, The 5-Fold Act of Divine Consciousness is; *Manifestation, Sustenance* (maintenance), *Withdrawal* (dissolution), *Concealment* and *Grace.*

What is the revelation of The 5-Fold Act of Divine Consciousness? The revelation of the 5-Fold Act is this; Taking the immanent aspect first, when you open your eyes upon waking in the morning and immediately perceive objects (people, places, things), this is Śiva's act of Manifestation. When you sustain those objects in your view (hold them in your perception) for a period of time, this is God's act of Sustenance. When you remove one object from your mind by replacing it with another, or when you remove objects from your mind, as when you close your eyes or otherwise turn away from those objects (as in Meditation), this is His act of Withdrawal.

When in the process of creating, sustaining and withdrawing the objects of your perception, you are not aware or you forget that you are Spanda Śakti; when you forget that you are The Self, God, this is Śiva-Śakti's act of Concealment. And when, during this same process of creating, sustaining and withdrawing objects, you have the realization that you are Śiva or you remember that you are that Supreme "I" Consciousness, this is His act of Grace.

In their *transcendental* aspect, these same 5 deeds are Śiva's act of Manifesting the Universe (involution); His act of Sustaining the Universe through His Will (Śakti); Śiva's act of Withdrawing or Dissolving the Universe at the end of each world cycle; His act of Concealing his true nature from himself (Māyā) so that the manifestation can continue to be; and His act of Grace (evolution) so that the Jīva (individual bound soul) can realize his/her union with Śiva-Śakti.

This is the *Play of Divine Consciousness* wherein Śiva takes all the forms and plays all the roles for his own sport. All of this occurs in the body of the Divine Lord, Anuttara. Thou Art That. With this as one's constant understanding, life is no longer an ocean of worldliness full of bondage and pitfalls, but a world full of God and His Love.

> *Śiva, the independent and pure Self that always*
> *vibrates in the mind, is the ParaŚakti that rises as*
> *joy in various sense experiences. Then the experience*
> *of this outer world appears as its Self. I do not know*
> *where this word 'samsara' has come from.*
>
> *Sri Abhinavagupta*

How To Use the Sūtras

The Sūtras On The 5-Fold Act of Divine Consciousness are laid out with separate sūtras for each of the 5 kṛtyas (deeds). There is a Prologue. The sūtras begin with the Prologue and this section is intended to set the overall tone of the work. There is also an Epilogue. The Sūtras conclude in the Epilogue and that section is intended to close the work.

There is a section of Dhāraṇās (contemplations or centering techniques) in the back of this book. These Dhāraṇās can be used before or after the reading of any of the Sūtras, as a means of contemplating the import of a Sūtra by way of making the mind quiet. They can also be used in preparation for sitting meditation. To contemplate means to steadily regard with your heart, without prejudging or forming premature notions about that which you are contemplating. These contemplations are designed to take you inside to the source of the teaching. Some of these Dhāraṇās are quotes or excerpts from the Āgamas and sacred texts of the Spanda School of Trika Śaivism.

When contemplating, do so with the absolute conviction that you, the contemplation itself and the One who is the underlying principle of the contemplation, are all one in the same.

Invocation

The following is an invocation to Lord Śiva written by Sadguru Kedarji.
These Sūtras are based on this invocation.

Om Śri Guru Mahādev

You are beyond this manifold Universe and have become everything in it.

You are the thought of a thought, the witness to all thoughts
The source of all thoughts, the rising and setting of all thoughts
And that which causes thought to emerge.

You are the taste in taste, you are the sight in sight
You are that which hears, you are the feeling in feeling
You are the one who smells.

Om Śri Guru Mahādev

You are the word in the words, the power behind the syllables,
The sound inherent in the power of those syllables,
The power behind the power in that sound
And the one who makes it possible to understand and to perceive.

You are the perception in perception, the Consciousness behind all
consciousness, the sense in sense pleasures and that which causes the
senses to perceive.

Yet you are also beyond the senses
And you are also the means of going beyond the senses.

Om Śri Guru Mahādev
Paśupati Guru Mahādev

You are both immanent and transcendental
And the one who gives meaning to the phrase immanent and
transcendental.

You become the object of all ideation, the object of all thought
And yet you are also not the objects that you become,
Reflecting those objects in your own being.

You are the one in the many and the many in the one.
You are Spanda Śakti, that power that manifests the perception
Of a world, the perception of a Universe.
Yet you have never taken birth and you have never died either.

Om Śri Guru Mahādev

You are the whisper behind the whisper that dissolves in the wind of the
fire that is contained in your heart; that same breath that creates, sustains
And withdraws the memory of existence in the body of your
consciousness.

You are the created, the uncreated and
That which is beyond the perception of all creation.

Om Śri Guru Mahādev
Paśupati Guru Mahādev

You are both real and unreal,
The awareness that gives birth to a Universe.

Like the child of a barren woman, there is no relationship between you
And that which manifests through your Chit Śakti.

And yet you thread through everything in this world,
So close, so intimate, and higher than any concept or notion can grasp.

Om Śri Guru Mahādev

Who are you? When the question dissolves the answer is Self-evident.
Behind all veils, you are the one pretending to hide.
Indeed, you become the very veil that you cover yourself with.
How beautiful is your play!

You are the one who removes the veil that you have cast on yourself
With your own hand, disguising yourself and revealing yourself
For your own amusement, while remaining the one who is the witness to it all.

Om Śri Guru Mahādev
Paśupati Guru Mahādev

One without a second, there can be no other.
What use is glory when you are behind it?
What use is time when you are the one behind it?
What use is pleasure when you are behind it?
What use is pain when you are the one behind it?

You make what cannot be fathomed readily experienced
by the awareness of your being.
By thinking of you, one experiences God.
By worshipping you, one becomes God.

The unreachable is reached by you. The unattainable is attained by you.
That which is unfathomable is easily ascertained by your awareness.
Once your are known, everything is known,
Even as you wander about as if knowing nothing.

Look, see there. You are everywhere, in everything and in everyone.

It is you who is looking
At the one who is looking.
It is you who is seeking
The one who is seeking.
Oh, how playful you arc!

Yasyonmesanimeṣābhyāṃ jagataḥ pralayo dayau /
Taṃ Śakticakravibhavaprabhavaṃ Śankaram stumaḥ // 1

We praise that Śankara (Śiva) who is the source of the Power of the Wheel of Energies by whose expansion (unmeṣa) and contraction (nimeṣa) the Universe is absorbed and comes into being.

Spanda-Kārikās 1.1

Prologue

There are no others. Only That One exists.

1. The Supreme Being, the Absolute One God is the power of Consciousness that illumines this entire Universe and all other worlds as well. That Supreme Consciousness is every thing.

2. There is only one path to God. That is the path that the Supreme Śiva Consciousness, God himself, travels along, in the form of his Śakti, to remove ignorance from one's being and to reveal the Heart which is the Supreme Being Himself. That path is known as the Suṣumnā Nādi or subtle body, a path every human being has within his/herself. All other paths are actually various approaches to making the mind fit to receive and embrace the Grace-bestowing power of God, in preparation for being led on this Siddha path.

3. The Suṣumnā path is the Siddha Path. Some say that Kuṇḍalinī Śakti travels along this Suṣumnā path to become unified with Lord Śiva. How can there be union when there is no separation? Śiva and Śakti are never separate. Separation is a perception of those ignorant of the Truth. The journey along the Siddha Path of Suṣumnā Nādi is undertaken by Śakti to reveal this Truth; that there is never any separation between Śiva and Śakti.

4. That Supreme Being or power of Consciousness can be known by awareness of The 5-Fold Act of Divine Consciousness (Pancakṛtya) or 5 deeds that this being performs constantly in a way that is uninterrupted.

5. These 5 Kṛtyas, known as The 5-Fold Act of Divine Consciousness, are Manifestation (creation), Sustenance, Withdrawal, Concealment and Grace. It is through this 5-Fold Act of Divine Consciousness that a Universe is perceived within the body of Supreme Consciousness. This 5-Fold Act is also the means by which one becomes aware that this Universe is a Play of Divine Consciousness.

6. Full awareness that this Universe is a Play of Divine Consciousness in which the Absolute is playing at all the roles brings the exalted state of Jīvanmukti in which, while still in the body, you realize that God alone exists. This realization is not intellectual. Upon having it, the realization becomes your very life and your life and lifestyle completely reflect this realization. In this way, you become the principle you have realized.

7. Owing to the existence of objects (people, places and things), we know there is a Supreme Being. The existence of objects is the proof of this higher power.

8.   Consciousness, in order to be Omniscient, Omnipotent and Omnipresent, must have two aspects. If these two aspects are not present, it cannot be said to be Consciousness. Therefore, the existence of these two aspects is what makes Consciousness Supreme because nothing exists outside of this Consciousness.

9.   The first is the aspect that causes the second to exist. One is the Supreme Śiva Consciousness (Universal God Consciousness or God-principle) and the other is the power of that Consciousness to cause objects to manifest.

10. Without the first aspect that is all-pervasive, the second aspect cannot exist, for existence itself is based on the power to perceive and that power belongs to the Perceiver, the Supreme Śiva (God) Consciousness.

11. By His power all things are known. Therefore who else can exist except the one by whose power all things are known and experienced?

12. For this reason, the One God that we call Lord Śiva, has two aspects; the transcendental and the immanent.

13. These two aspects are like a subject and its reflection. The Supreme Subject is always reflecting Himself. The reflecting surface is what causes the subject to appear as if different and full of diversity when, in fact, He is one in the same player.

14. This very diversity is a perception created by this Supreme Subject (Śiva Consciousness) within His own being.

15. This diversity would seem to be full of duality but, in fact, it is not. It is perceived to be so due to the reflecting surface (the object) which He Himself has become.

16. That which reflects like a mirror is not separate from the Lord. The reflecting surface, and its variations, are all contained in the same body of Supreme Consciousness.

17. Therefore, all objects (people, places and things) are reflected inside the body of this Supreme Śiva Consciousness.

18. The reflection is this Universe. That is His Play.

19. Like an actor, when the Supreme Being covers himself in one way, we call it the waking state. When He puts on another covering or costume, we call it dreaming. When He covers himself again in a different way, we call it deep sleep and when he reveals that He is just playing, that is the awareness beyond these three states.

20. Our life experience is manifested through these coverings that He wears like an actor wears a costume.

21. When the awareness that it is God who is acting as the objects of this world-appearance becomes permanent, that is Samādhi or Liberation.

22. This awareness becomes permanent through the realization that each of us is engaged in this, His Play of Divine Consciousness, because we perform the same five Divine acts (or deeds) as God does when He plays at becoming this entire manifestation.

23. The Supreme Being, Lord Śiva has five infinite powers through which He manifests the coverings (his costumes) that allow him to disguise Himself as an actor does.

24. He disguises himself so that he can convincingly play all the roles in this manifold existence.

25. From these five infinite powers, the Absolute Universal Being of Supreme Consciousness manifests as the activity of this world. This manifestation occurs through His active, divine energy of Consciousness that is called Śakti. This Śakti is also known as Kaulikī or Kaulinī because she manifests the entire wheel or grouping of energies known as Kula. The Kula includes the 36 Tattvas or stages of manifestation of this Universe.

26. Without this Śakti of Śiva, these five infinite powers cannot reflect anything.

27. These five infinite powers are Being-Awareness (Chit), Bliss (Ānanda), Divine Will/Divine Intellect (Icchā), Direct Knowledge of the Absolute (Jñāna) and the Perception of Activity or Purposeless Action (Kriyā).

28. By His scintillating, glamorous Chit or Spanda Śakti (Śakti of Śiva), these five infinite powers contract to become the very stage that this world-appearance takes place on.

29. From these five infinite powers, He manifests, of His own sweet will, five actions that He himself engages in for His own sport and entertainment. These five deeds form the dramatic script in which this Play of Divine Consciousness is found.

30. These five deeds are known as The 5-Fold Act of Divine Consciousness.

31. The Supreme Being creates the entire Universe within His own body of Supreme Consciousness.

32. He then sustains all the worlds within His Śiva Consciousness.

33. After relishing His creation in this way, Śiva withdraws the entire cosmos (all 118 Universes) inside His own body of Supreme Consciousness and dissolves all perception of activity there.

34. In order to play, in order to act as a consummate actor would, the Supreme Being conceals His true identity.

35. Just as a great actor does not let on that he/she is just acting, the Supreme Lord acts as each and every person, place and thing in this Universe, while concealing His true nature.

36. When He reveals that He is just acting and that His true identity, His true nature has never changed, that is His act of Grace.

37. His Śakti is The Player in this world-appearance, as in this entire Universe. This is also His act of Grace.

38. This all-pervasive Śakti, herself becomes the internal soul that exists freely and independently in all forms of objects, both sentient and insentient.

39. This internal soul also performs the same 5-Fold Act that the Supreme Being performs.

40. In this way, His Śakti enacts this very Play of Divine Consciousness that is His dance.

41. This dance is a drama.

THE SŪTRAS ON MANIFESTATION

THE SŪTRAS ON MANIFESTATION

42. Welling up out of His pure joy, this entire Universe comes into being.

43. Descending in an arc of Light, Spanda becomes the subtlest of the subtle. Then, forming a straight line of pure gold and taking her form of golden Light, the Goddess Spanda Śakti dances back and forth in pure delight between two points (visarga), becoming this very Manifestation inside and out.

44. Sound is inherent in Light, and Light in Sound. Springing forth together, the Creation is thus formed out of what already exists in his own being.

45. From the Light that is its own power source (Prakāśa), the Supreme Śiva manifests a vibration (Vimarśa). From that vibration comes sound. And from that sound, He causes the letters already contained within Himself to manifest.

46. The Lord's Divine Conscious Energy, His Śakti (Spanda) creates her own reflection in the objects of this world so that the Absolute can survey Himself.

47. This vibration takes on the nature of awareness of distinctions. In this way it manifests as 50 perceptions. These perceptions are phonemes and these phonemes become the objects. This is how external objects manifest in the body of Supreme Consciousness.

48. The illusion of the existence of a world, a Universe, is Manifestation. And Manifestation is the illusion that a world actually exists.

49. This very illusion, known as Śiva's Māyā or Māyā Śakti, is neither real or unreal. And yet She appears to be both real and unreal. That is His genius.

50. Out of what exists in His own being, Śiva creates this world through

his own Vimarśa (Spanda Śakti) and manifests a Universe comprised of this very energy of Light and Sound.

51. Human beings, owing to their being comprised of this very same Vimarśa aspect, and this very same Prakāśa aspect, also create their own world, which is then Superimposed on to God.

52. The mind is the creative contraction of Śiva-Śakti, of God.

53. By manifesting letters, the Supreme Being creates words, and from those words come sentences. This is our language.

54. Language is Manifestation. This is the principle of Vak in our Shaivism.

55. Language undergoes three stages of Manifestation that unfold out of the highest vibration (sometimes also referred to as a stage of manifestation). The understanding of this illusion we call world is inherent in these three stages of Manifestation we call language.

56. The highest vibration is called Parā or Paravak. This Parā is sometimes referred to as the first stage of the manifestation of language but Parā is actually the cause of the other three stages, being contained equally in each. So, we do not call it a stage since it is the energy substratum of all. Parā is the sound that exists as the seed form of letters before those letters actually manifest. This is a vibration (Spanda) that is in a state of readiness to manifest as letters.

57. The next stage of the manifestation of language or speech, in descending order (meaning less subtle), is Paśyantī. Paśyantī is the subtle manifestation of letters, before they are recognizable as such, meaning that the letters are not yet distinguishable from the vibration of sound. They are experienced as a sensation only.

58. The next stage of the manifestation of language (more gross) is Madhyamā. Madhyamā is the level of subtle speech where letters begin to become fully formed.

59. The last (third) stage of the manifestation of language is Vaikharī. Vaikharī is the level of gross speech where letters are blatant and manifest as words and sentences.

60. Because these letters, words and sentences manifest out of God's Supreme energy of Divine Consciousness (Śakti), letters, words and sentences are this same Supreme energy of Divine Consciousness known as Śiva's Chiti or Śakti.

61. All letters, words and sentences manifest from this same source, Chit Śakti, and dissolve back into this same source. Therefore, every word is a Mantra with a host of understandings connected to it.

62. Because language has, as its source, this Supreme energy of Divine Consciousness, words, letters and sentences have the power to alter perceptions by manifesting the understandings that cause emotions to rise within you. This is due to God's power of Supreme Consciousness.

63. By this language, the Goddess Spanda or Chiti, causes thought to manifest. In fact, she becomes all thoughts by way of these mantras.

64. The movement in Divine Consciousness, called the mind, is the Superimposition of this Universe on to the Pure Perceiving Awareness.

65. When this Śakti of Śiva causes language to manifest, the mind manifests ('mind' itself is a mantra). It is this Chiti that takes the form of the mind (Chitta).

66. In this way, Śiva's Śakti witnesses the mind as it weaves one thought, desire, notion, concept, belief and emotion after another.

67. The one who witnesses the mind is the Revealer of this Act. It is that Revealer who creates, who manifests all the Universes.

68. Śakti causes these thoughts to rise and fall, to manifest and disintegrate. This is her dance.

69. The sound inherent in the letters of the alphabet is God. The person who understands this endeavors in the Manifestation by exercising wise and careful choices in the vibration she creates through the language she uses.

70. All of Manifestation begins with the inward breath that sounds the sacred syllable as Prāṇa enters the body.

71. You, the individual bound soul, perform the same act of Manifestation that the Lord performs. Thought is this act of Manifestation.

72. Due to God's power, you have the ability to manifest thought and that thought is an object (person, place or thing) within the body of Supreme Consciousness where this Earth plane and all other planes exist.

73. By superimposing a thought, notion, desire or craving on to the body of Supreme Śiva Consciousness, you project something that you have experienced elsewhere on to your internal screen.

74. This act of projecting is your act of Manifestation. It is how you yourself perform the first of the 5-Fold Act of Divine Consciousness known as Manifestation. When you are aware that you do this, you become one with the Revealer.

75. Without the complete realization of God, this Manifestation becomes a limiting, binding illusion that causes you to be bounced back and forth between pleasure and pain.

76. All of Manifestation is reflective awareness. Each one must understand this for oneself.

THE SŪTRAS ON SUSTENANCE

THE SŪTRAS ON SUSTENANCE

77. Creating Viṣṇu, the deity of Sustenance, Śiva-Śakti maintains this manifestation for the purpose of the free evolution of beings. The goal of this evolution is absorption into Divine Love. This is His sport.

78. Taking the form of Śiva's activity, His immanent aspect, Lord Viṣṇu Sustains this world through Śiva's consort or grouping of Śaktis, also known as Kula. These Śaktis; Ghorā, Mahāghora and Aghora, sustain this Play of Divine Consciousness by casting down, again and again, those who have no longing for God; and by raising up those who long for The Absolute alone.

79. Contracting to become all 36 Tattvas, from Pṛthvī (Earth) up to Parama Śiva (the Absolute), Lord Viṣṇu, himself a manifestation of Śiva, becomes the mala-covered samsārin and all sentient and insentient beings.

80. Through three of His Śaktis or powers, Icchā (Divine Will), Jñāna (Supreme Knowledge) and Kriyā (Purposeless Action), the great Lord Śiva sustains this universe of forms by contracting to become the very limited will, limited knowledge and limited (tainted) action of the individual bound soul. In this way, that which is unreal, uncreated and formless is perceived to be real through the 36 Tattvas or stages of manifestation. Among these tattvas is The City of Eight (the subtle body or Suṣumnā Nādi) that is responsible for the sustenance of this Play of Divine Consciousness.

81. Through His Divine Power, Spanda Śakti, also known as His active aspect (Vimarśa), that great Lord Śiva manifests himself as The City of Eight in order to sustain this universe. This City of Eight is the individual intellect, the ego, the mind, and the five senses, along with their offspring. These are known as the tanmātras, karmendriyas, jñānendriyas and antaḥkaraṇas in our Shaivism.

82. By concealing His true nature, Śiva-Śakti, the God Principle within causes this City of Eight to be perceived as the only reality, thereby engaging human beings in thought (action) that they attribute to the body.

83. This world-appearance is sustained. It's continued existence makes this fact obvious. This entire Universe in which this world-appearance is contained is also sustained. This act of Sustenance (or maintenance) is performed by the One who reveals this Act. The Revealer is the sustainer of this Universe.

84. Who is this revealer? He is the one who sees through your eyes, hears through your ears, feels through your body and emotions and smells through your nose. The Revealer takes the form of your senses in order to sustain this world-appearance.

85. Conscious energy is everything. This Conscious energy we call Śakti or Chiti. It is also called the Vibration of Divine Consciousness known as Spanda. Activity only exists because it is perceived to exist and without this Śakti of Śiva, nothing can be perceived anywhere.

86. The ability to perceive objects is also His power of Sustenance.

87. This Vibration of Divine Consciousness of Śiva, called Spanda or Chiti, is engaged in creating the perception of a Universe that is full of diversity and duality. As the active power (Vimarśa) of Śiva Consciousness, she is always manifesting, sustaining and dissolving countless worlds, by manifesting perceptions within the body of the Supreme Being.

88. Sustenance is desire. Śiva-Śakti, through the will (Saṅkalpa) of the individual, takes the form of all intention, thereby securing the existence of a universe through the perception of "doership."

89. This "doership" is the creative contraction of the Supreme "I" Consciousness into the limited "I" consciousness of the individual.

90. Concealing his true nature, that great Lord goes about his daily existence, considering what is unreal to be completely real and separate from himself.

91. Through the creation of Kārmas, this Play of Divine Consciousness is sustained by the perception of a mere world.

92. His Wheel of Energies (Śaktis) contract to become the sound inherent in the letters of the alphabet that form language. Language is the basis for the Sustenance of Māyā, that which causes Supreme Consciousness to be measured out in a contracted and limited way.

93. This world-appearance expands through the understandings and perceptions created by letters, words and sentences. It is Śakti herself who takes the form of language through these letters, words and sentences. She is the power of sound inherent in these.

94. When Śakti takes the form of language, she is called Mātṛikā Śakti or Mātṛukā, the un-understood mother of Śiva's Māyā.

95. Through the power of Mātṛikā, the perception of objects is created and then sustained.

96. These objects (people, places and things) are merely reflections of the Supreme Subject, the Absolute or Ultimate Reality. Mātṛikā is the power that reflects these objects in Consciousness.

97. Words have power because God is in the words. Language has the ability to alter your perception and view of this world because Mātṛikā Śakti is the root of all language.

98. God is the power behind each letter and syllable. This is why words have so much power over you.

99. When the limitation of your ego is allowed to expand through your use of language, Mātṛikā becomes the force that keeps you bound to worldliness and ignorance of the Truth.

100. When the limitation of your ego is destroyed through your use of language (mantra), Mātṛikā becomes the force that Liberates you from the ignorance you have created, by revealing God to you.

101. Because this is the case, she (Mātṛikā) is all-powerful. This is so because perception of an object, perception of form is only possible

through letters, words and sentences and Mātṛikā is the creator of those letters, words and sentences.

102. From language comes thought, understandings, notions, ideas, concepts and beliefs. From these rise desire and craving. From desire and craving come worldliness and the multitudinous fantasies of this fantasmagorical existence. Mātṛikā Śakti is the root of all this. It is she who sustains this world-appearance.

103. Mātṛikā manifests due to Śiva's Māyā. This Māyā Śakti is the power of Sustenance. She sustains by concealing the Truth.

104. You, the individual bound soul, perform the same act of Sustenance that the Lord performs. When you sustain a particular thought or notion in your mind, when you ruminate over a person, place or thing, you are performing His act of Sustenance.

105. By engaging your senses, you also perform this same act of Sustenance.

106. Through attachment to the senses and objects of sense, through becoming entangled in the play of your senses, you also perform this act of Sustenance.

107. The Revealer is the one who masquerades as your form, with a body, a name, a career, a car, a house, a lover and so on.

108. The one who comes and goes through cycle after cycle of birth and death is the Revealer of this act of Sustenance.

109. By the play of your senses, your mind becomes attached to objects (people, places and things). By way of this attachment, you continue to ruminate over these objects in your mind. In this way, you continue to perform this act of Sustenance, even in the dream state.

110. In this way, this Play of Divine Consciousness that is this world-appearance, is sustained by you.

THE SŪTRAS ON WITHDRAWAL

THE SŪTRAS ON WITHDRAWAL

111. After a time of sporting as Spanda (Chit Śakti) in this Play of Divine Consciousness, He, the Divine Consciousness (Lord Śiva) withdraws this entire universe, reabsorbing it into himself. There he rests in himself for some time and then another cycle of manifestation, sustenance and withdrawal begins.

112. Corresponding to the four ages, one world cycle takes place, after which He reabsorbs all objects into himself, resting there for a time until He projects himself outward once again to begin the next world cycle.

113. These four ages, representing one world cycle, are: Satya Yuga, Treta Yuga, Dvāpara Yuga and Kālī Yuga.

114. As these four ages progress, Dharma (Righteousness) declines as evil begins to overcome good. At the end of Kālī Yuga, the Supreme Being withdraws all worlds and universes back into himself and there is no perception of objects within the body of Supreme Consciousness and, therefore, no activity either.

115. Śiva causes the Universe to vibrate between two points. These points are represented as an upper point and a lower point. Spanda Śakti contracts and expands between these two points in an endless cycle. Movement away from the lower point back to the upper point is Withdrawal. It is this movement that causes the universe to be reabsorbed or withdrawn into His being for a time.

116. In withdrawal, Śakti moves away from objects of its own sense perception, turning inward on itself and, eventually, withdrawing all perception of activity into Śiva.

117. Expanding from the tattvas of materiality, this Spanda Śakti withdraws all 36 Tattvas, dissolving each into the preceding one, until it comes to rest in the eternal Anuttara, the eternal Absolute, once again.

118. You, the individual soul, also perform this act of Withdrawal on a daily basis in a limited way.

119. The Supreme Subject, who takes the form of the internal soul, has five states of Consciousness in the physical body. These states are known as Jāgrat (wakefulness or the waking state), Svapna (dreaming or the dream state), Suṣupti (the state of deep sleep), Turya (the state beyond the first three) and Turyātīta (the state beyond Turya). Within each of the first four states (Jāgrat, Svapna, Suṣupti and Turya) there exists four levels or coverings that can also be called Jāgrat, Svapna, Suṣupti and Turya (Ex: jāgrat-jāgrat, jāgrat-svapna, jāgrat-suṣupti, jāgrat-turya, etc.)

120. When the Supreme Subject travels in objectivity and becomes the object by ignoring its Śiva Consciousness, this is the waking state or covering known as Jāgrat, meaning wakefulness.

121. When this same Supreme Subject or Śiva Consciousness travels in the cognitive world while forgetting it's true nature, and without becoming any object of perception, this is the dream state or covering known as Svapna, meaning dreaming.

122. When the Supreme Subject travels in the subjective world without being conscious of its nature as the Absolute, this is the covering known as Suṣupti, the state of deep sleep.

123. When this same Supreme Subject travels in Śiva Consciousness and becomes Śiva Consciousness, this is the fourth state called Turya.

124. When the Supreme Subject becomes fully re-established in that state of the Absolute or Śiva Consciousness, this is known as Turyātīta, meaning the state beyond the fourth.

125. When you divert your conscious awareness from one object of sense that is in your physical (external) presence to another, you are engaged in His act of Withdrawal.

126. When you withdraw your awareness from the waking state

entirely but continue to ruminate over the impressions left behind on your mind by those objects, you are traveling through the world of your inner impressions (cognitive world). In this way, you perform His act of Withdrawal (withdrawal from Jāgrat into Svapna).

127. When you divert your awareness from Svapna (the world of your inner impressions) and enter into the state of the void, and you are not aware of anything whatsoever, you are engaged in His act of Withdrawal (you have withdrawn into deep sleep).

128. When you establish your awareness in the state of Turya, the state beyond the first three, and you are conscious of being aware but you have no thoughts, you perform His act of Withdrawal.

129. There is a witness to each of these levels of Withdrawal that you perform. That witness is who you really are.

THE SŪTRAS ON CONCEALMENT

THE SŪTRAS ON CONCEALMENT

130. Concealing His true nature through his group of Śaktis known as The Wheel of Energies, He becomes all sentient and insentient objects (people, places and things). In a living being, Śiva's Māyā is active through The City of Eight and the Tattvas, that vehicle that He uses to conceal his very nature in order to sport about playing all the roles, of His own free will. This is His sport, His play, His picnic, His entertainment in The Play of Divine Consciousness that He himself has created by way of the Goddess, Spanda Śakti. This act of concealment is God's shadow, His reflection inside His own being.

131. Even in this act of concealment, Spanda remains true to her own nature as Pure Perceiving Awareness.

132. Śiva-Śakti, that Divine God-principle, conceals itself in successive stages of limitation.

133. Māyā means "illusion." It also means "to measure out." The Supreme Śiva Consciousness decides to "scire" himself. In order to do so, this God-consciousness becomes an actor, concealing its true nature to others, just as an actor conceals that he/she is acting by playing a role magnificently.

134. The manifestation of this world-appearance is God's great act of Concealment. This act of concealment is a dance that is a Play of Divine Consciousness.

135. The Dancer is an actor and this world-appearance is the enchanting play of the actor of the Universe.

136. His power of reflection is His magnificent, glamorous Spanda Śakti.

137. Through His glamorous, scintillating Spanda Śakti, Lord Śiva conceals his true identity by manifesting as a plant, a tree, a person, an insect, a location, a car, a building, etc. In this way, the Supreme Being becomes all sentient and insentient objects.

138. This, His act of Concealment, is also Śiva's Māyā. This Māyā is His immanent aspect.

139. All beings, people, places, things, worlds and universes exist within Śiva's Māyā.

140. This Māyā is known to be an illusion because it is the Supreme Śiva Consciousness who is acting all the roles we experience in this world-appearance. Just as we don't mistake an actor who is playing all the roles in a comedy for the characters that one actor is playing, we should understand that objects are not separate or different from the great Lord, but rather they are His costumes, the ways in which He covers Himself.

141. In this Māyā, Superimposition is the means by which the Goddess Spanda Śakti conceals her true nature, weaving a grand tapestry of illusion without beginning or end.

142. In Superimposition, memory becomes the contracting force of concealment that, at first, binds the individual bound soul to ignorance, casting the Jīva down over and over again.

143. In this Superimposition, the senses interact with Buddhi, Ahaṃkāras and Manas to make the Jīva run back and forth between a pair of opposites. This pair of opposites is Pain and Pleasure. Together, these two are responsible for the drama of life that keeps the very act of Concealment concealed.

144. The journey to Pain and Pleasure is further concealed by language. The power of Mātrikā Śakti, inherent in the letters of the alphabet, further serves to cast a veil over the Ultimate Reality.

145. Lord Śiva creates this Māyā and conceals His true nature by becoming the very stage that this Māyā is enacted on. Parāmśiva becomes the costumes, the lights, the curtain, the stage hands, the sound equipment, the sound crew, the actors, the playwright, the producers, the director and the audience. If these are all one in the same Player, how can they be separate from Him?

146. This world-appearance manifests due to His act of Concealment. The Revealer is also the one who conceals.

147. The free will of the individual further serves to conceal God's true nature through the creation of Kārma.

148. The illusion known as Śiva's Māyā is sustained through the Karmashaya (pot of Kārmas). In this way, concealment of the Supreme Reality, Śiva, is guaranteed.

149. The ego is the seat of concealment that limits the individual's pure nature through the creation of Kārmas. This ego becomes vast and subtle through the fuel known as limiting desire and craving.

150. You, the individual bound soul, also perform this act of Concealment.

151. When you experience an event in which you are terrified, sick, uncomfortable or angry, and, through the passing of time you feel that you have gotten over it, only to find years later that you suddenly remember the event and re-experience the event within your being, that is your act of Concealment. (The event you thought you had gotten over was merely concealed within you.)

152. When you choose to behave counter to how you know you should behave, or counter to what your conscience is telling you, you perform this act of Concealment.

153. When you forget or become ignorant of the fact that you are God and that the Supreme Being, the Absolute, dwells within you as you, this is His act of Concealment.

154. When you don't know that you are the Śiva-Śakti principle and that you are just playing, acting the role of your form, you are concealing your true nature from yourself. This is His act of Concealment.

155. Śiva Consciousness becomes the senses and all that is perceived through the senses, in order to conceal the fact that this world-appearance is an illusion brought on by His Māyā Śakti.

156. The Revealer is hidden, concealed. Through attachment to the senses

and their objects, you lose your awareness of the Revealer. This is your act of Concealment.

157. The One, Absolute Śiva Consciousness becomes the objects that thought produces. Therefore, this One Revealer is the power of ideation. These objects are reflections of this Supreme Śiva that manifest in the body of Supreme Śiva Consciousness. The One Revealer is not the objects He reflects. Śiva remains Śiva even as Śiva becomes the objects being reflected in Consciousness. This is His act of Concealment.

158. When The City of Eight (the Suṣumnā Nadi) is purified and the ego is renounced completely, God reveals himself, thereby ending the cycle of concealment.

THE SŪTRAS ON GRACE

THE SŪTRAS ON GRACE

159. It is God's Grace that leads you to the Master, known as a Siddha or Shaktipat Sadguru, who is the grace-bestowing power of God and a true spiritual leader. And it is that Sadguru's Grace that sets you on your own path back to God. Grace is the beginning, the middle and the end. Nothing can be accomplished without Grace.

160. Grace is the reason you breathe. Grace causes this Universe to come into being. It is through Grace that all the forms exist. It is by Grace that the cycle of birth and death exists eternally. And it is by Grace that the miracle of Grace is realized. Truly, there is nothing else.

161. To recognize Grace at work requires a subtle discrimination. To acknowledge Grace as the sole support of one's life requires an even greater discrimination. Such discrimination only comes with spiritual practice that will carry you to the very seat of Grace. And such spiritual practice can only be learned from a Sadguru, from a Master who has realized the goal of that practice. It is by Grace that you learn to experience and choose the transcendental over the immanent by looking for and recognizing the transcendental in the immanent. It is through the Supreme understanding of these two aspects that the group of energies of His immanent aspect is transformed by surrendering to its true nature.

162. Grace is the Master. Of this there is no doubt.

163. Revelation is Grace. It is the awareness of God's act of Concealment, the awareness that the Supreme Being conceals Himself.

164. There are not millions of individual souls engaged in action and experience. There is only one Universal Experient, One Supreme Being who takes the form of all the internal souls, becoming every "individual," every "place" and every "thing."

165. Grace is the direct perception of this One Universal Experient in the many.

166. When the Revealer, the One Supreme Being, reveals the fact that it is He who conceals Himself as the activity of this world, as the form of this entire Universe, that is called Grace.

167. Grace is the awareness that the perception of this world-appearance is the power of Grace. For who can give the power to perceive anything, except the Revealer of that power.

168. The One who acts as if it is a human form, a plant, a tree, a lake, the ocean, a rock, an animal, etc. is the author of this world-appearance. That is called Chiti, Spanda or Śakti and That is the power of the Revealer, Lord Śiva.

169. Lord Śiva and His Śakti are not two. They are One. This is the revelation of Grace.

170. Through this Grace a seeker understands the Truth; Consciousness is everything. This Supreme Śiva Consciousness has never taken birth and it never dies. Only the perception of forms takes birth and dies. The Revealer of all forms, that One who creates, sustains and withdraws this manifold Universe, is the only one who exists. Direct knowledge of this fact is Grace.

171. Knowledge of the Player, the One who becomes the sport of this Play of Divine Consciousness we call "world," direct knowledge and experience of this Player is Grace.

172. The Player is the Author and Revealer of this Play of Divine Consciousness. That is the same one who plays at all the forms that are the "characters" of this world-appearance. It is by His power that one sees the magnificence of the play. That power is His Grace.

173. Even the act of revelation by a "Revealer" is just an act because, in truth, the revealer never conceals himself from himself. The constant awareness of this fact is Grace.

174. Śiva-Śakti becomes the senses. In fact, your senses are the vehicles of That.

They are the tools that are used by Śiva Consciousness to enact this Play of Divine Consciousness.

175. You, the individual bound soul, also perform God's Act of Grace.

176. Only that power that is beyond the senses can become the senses. The Supreme Śiva-Śakti principle, also known as the Guru-principle, is that power. When your awareness rises beyond the perceiving ability of your senses, when you understand that Śiva-Śakti is also the means of going beyond the senses, you are engaged in God's act of Grace.

177. When you remember that you are that Śiva Consciousness that perceives your being and perceives through your being, you perform God's act of Grace.

178. Letters, words and sentences are all indicators of aspects of Śiva-Śakti. These various and multitudinous aspects of God all exist inside the body of Supreme Consciousness. When you maintain the awareness of this fact, even as you go about your daily mundane activities, this is God's act of Grace.

179. You are the immanent aspect of the Lord. When you realize this fact and then align yourself with it, you are engaged in God's act of Grace.

180. When you are aware that it is you who is performing this act, you become one with the Revealer.

181. When you choose to engage the virtues, such as unconditional Love, Compassion, Patience, Forbearance, Peace, Gratitude and Selfless Service, you perform God's act of Grace.

182. When you place the common good above your own personal needs and desires, you are engaged in God's act of Grace.

183. When, through the Grace of a Sadguru, you choose to sublimate your will to merge in God's Will, you perform God's act of Grace.

184. The depth, power and benefit of Grace is unfathomable. This is

because Grace is at work constantly, even when the seeker is not aware of it.

185. To become aware of Grace is to understand and experience this world-appearance as His two aspects, the Immanent and the Transcendental.

186. Just as the wind cannot be seen, and yet we can experience its effects all around us and we know of its existence in this way; so too Grace, although mysterious and working in ways that often cannot be understood, is immanent everywhere.

187. Even though Grace is the support of this entire world-appearance, in order for it's transforming power to be realized, the seeker must learn to recognize its presence.

188. The recognition of the presence of Grace is established through Śaktipat, the spiritual awakening bestowed upon the seeker by the an authentic Shaktipat Guru.

189. The Grace of such a Sadguru is constantly at work within the disciple even though he/she may not be aware of it. It is in the giving, as well as in the taking away.

190. This Grace never stops working on behalf of the disciple's ultimate transformation and well-being, even though there may be times when it may not appear to be at work at all.

191. This Grace, once bestowed, never goes to waste. However, it is best capitalized on through the discipline, devotion and steady spiritual practice of the disciple. This is disciple's Grace. It enables the disciple to actually "steal," as it were, the Master's Śakti, the Guru's energy.

192. Although ultimately at work as the cause and the effect of this entire universe, Grace does not truly descend on a conscious person until the seeker makes the decision to orient his/her will toward God. It is in this act of setting the ego aside that the seeker attracts the Grace-bestowing power of God to his/herself.

193. Although recognizable by an individual in certain moments of distress, although recognizable by the devotee in certain moments of compassion and honor, although recognizable by a person in certain moments of complete openness and surrender, the profound workings of Grace are best taken advantage of through the effort put forth for daily spiritual practice. In this way, a person orients his/her entire will to that path created and sustained by Grace.

194. Grace comes from a Master and the path is the Master's command and instruction.

195. In order to get wet, you have to get into the water. In order to cross a river, you have to get into the river. In order to be supported and transformed by Grace, you have to place yourself firmly in this ever-flowing path of Grace. Discipleship is the means by which this occurs.

196. Although inherent in every activity of this world due to God being immanent in everything and everyone, the flow of Grace to the individual only becomes steady through steadfast love for God, through steadfast love for humanity, through steadfast love for the living Sadguru.

197. Although wish-fulfilling, the highest form of Grace is that which purifies the disciple, causing one to merge his/her entire identity into God, into Śiva.

198. It is Grace that instills the understanding that the body is nothing more than a means to fulfilling the goal of all life by merging with the Absolute.

199. Armed with Grace, you are able to immediately recognize Śiva's transcendental and immanent aspects at play in every moment of your life.

200. It is Grace that gives you the ability to recognize that you have a choice in choosing the transcendental over the immanent.

201. Through Grace you learn the Witness Consciousness of a Siddha and, by doing so, you learn to deposit craving, compulsion and desire all in one

place, in the fire of Grace that is awakened inside your own being by the Master.

202. It is through Grace that the mind becomes quiet, turning in on itself to become Chiti once again.

203. Grace is the agent by which the ego and the senses are purified in the fire of the Sadguru's unceasing Love.

204. What is Grace? Grace is seeking out the one who gives it.

205. What is Grace? Grace is receiving Grace in a way that gives you the ultimate experience of Grace.

206. What is the ultimate experience of Grace? The ultimate experience of Grace is the awareness that it is you who pervades all people, places and things. You are God and God is you. Therefore, God exists in everything and everyone, everywhere, equally.

207. The proof of Grace at work is everywhere. It is in your breathing, seeing, speaking, smelling, tasting, touching and feeling. It is in your every action. The proof of Grace is in your emotions. It is in your very ability to roam in the pleasure-garden of this world-appearance. The proof of Grace at work is in nature, in the rivers, in the ocean, in the mountains with their trees, in the forest on the high plains and low plains, in the cities, in the high-rise buildings, in the malls, as well as in the villages and cottages.

208. This proof of Grace is your very existence. There is no other miracle required. Grace itself is all this and that which causes all this to be. It is eternal without a second and it will remain whether the universe continues to be or not.

209. Even the doubt that may exist in your mind as to its very existence is due to His Divine Grace. Otherwise who is it that recognizes doubt as such and how could such a thing ever be recognized? Grace exists and is recognized by Grace. It is none other than the Supreme Śiva-Śakti principle at play.

Epilogue

210. God has two aspects; one is the immanent aspect and the other is transcendental.

211. Constant awareness of these two aspects is vital for spiritual growth.

212. Existence is a memory. How can one who has never taken birth exist now? So, existence itself is an illusion. However, there is a trick to it. That One who remembers that existence is an illusion, That One actually exists. And because That One exists, the Universe exists. You see how great His play is? By the Grace of the Guru, the mind finally realizes that it cannot figure it out. When this realization dawns, the mind becomes quiet. In that silence existence is understood for what it really is.

213. How can words bring knowledge of the Absolute? They cannot. Just as a map of a region is not the region itself but just a map, words can only indicate the reflection of the Absolute. When there are no words, awareness of the Absolute reveals itself.

214. The Supreme Śiva Consciousness is both transcendental and immanent. This is so only because it is that one Absolute Supreme Being who gives meaning to the words "transcendental" and "immanent."

215. In the body of all creatures, Śiva comes and goes on Prāṇa or Prāṇa Śakti. This Prāṇa creates, sustains and withdraws the memory of existence in the body of your consciousness. For this reason, it can be called the internal soul.

216. This internal soul is a reflection of that which is beyond the perception of all manifestation, sustenance and withdrawal.

217. To become completely aware of the Supreme Subject who is the one reflected in the body of Supreme Consciousness as this world-appearance, you need the guidance and instruction of a person who has become one with the Revealer, the Supreme Śiva.

218. Talk is cheap. Awareness is everything. The Supreme Awareness

comes about through practice of the instruction given by a perfected Master of Yoga who is a Shaktipat Sadguru.

219. Although such a being can be called "Siddha," "Guru," "Acharya," "Master," "Swami," "Sri," etc., such a being is beyond such titles and, therefore, cannot be known by such words.

220. Such a being is known by the principles he/she has become and by whether or not you have a direct experience of God in his/her company and are being properly led by example through true spiritual leadership, not just words.

221. Such a being is known by his/her ability to fully awaken the dormant spiritual energy inside you, known as Kuṇḍalinī Śakti. This awakening is called Śaktipat.

222. Such a being can be known by his/her ability to instruct you and to lead you in a daily spiritual practice that is the means of attaining his/her state, the Supreme Self.

223. Such a being is one who has made the journey that you intend to make and has intimate, direct knowledge of its pitfalls, milestones and culmination.

224. Such a being will invoke within you the desire to know God and to merge with God. Just by keeping the company of such a being, you will want to become pure.

225. Follow only one who has crossed the ocean of worldliness and has left off ALL attachments to sense pleasures and worldly pleasures. Follow only one who has no expectation of these. Only such a being can lead you. Choose such a one very carefully.

226. Although seemingly many, such a being is rare. When you find such a Sadguru, keep *both* your feet in his house.

227. Such a being is the means. Such a being is the path. Such a being is God. To know Śiva is to understand His teaching and this is His teaching. To know Bhagawān Nityānanda is to understand His teaching and this is His teaching.

228. The Sadguru and the devotee are one. The Sadguru and disciple are one. This is the law. You are looking at the one who is looking. It is you who are seeking the one who is seeking.

There are no others. Only That One exists.

Agādhasaṃśayāmbhodhi-samuttaraṇatāriṇīm /
Vande vicitrārthapadāṃ citrāṃ tāṃ gurubhāratīm // 1

I pay homage to that wonderful instruction of my Guru that is like a boat for crossing the fathomless ocean of doubt and is full of words that yield wonderful meaning.

I offer my praise to *Spanda* which has taken the form of *Parā Vāk*, the Supreme I-Consciousness of Śiva in the form of the language of this teaching that is full of transcendental bliss, and is also the means by which I am carried across the ocean of worldliness to continually experience my essential nature as *Spanda*.

Spanda-Kārikās 4.1

Being Consciousness of Your Vibration

In Nityananda Shaktipat Yoga, one of the intentions of our spiritual practice is to become more conscious of how each of us is vibrating so that we can consciously infuse all our actions with the highest Vibration of Divine Consciousness, so that our thoughts and actions reflect our true nature, the Self.

In our every day mundane activities we experience many people, places and things and, as a result, we come into contact with a variety of different energies. Some of these we like and respect and others we don't. Then, in the course of these activities, we also experience things that we find distasteful and people, places and things that we would like to change.

Very often we can observe that those who have made perceived changes have really only duplicated, in some way, those things they wished to change. This is especially true of changes in personal behavior and social/societal change. For example, people who fight against social injustice often become like and use the same tactics as those they are fighting against. In order to avoid emotional pain ourselves, we inflict emotional pain on others. In order to quench our thirst, we steal someone else's water.

In Nityananda Shaktipat Yoga, we make the constant effort to become more aware of what each of us, individually, is putting out (projecting into Consciousness). We make the constant effort to become more aware of how we can take greater responsibility for our own individual actions so that we can be ever aware of how we are vibrating. *Change is meaningless if we become like those people, places and things that we are seeking to change or improve.* **This is why we say the best change is for you to become more conscious of how you are vibrating and what you are putting out or projecting into manifestation. The best change you can make in this world and for this world is to change yourself.** This becomes an easy task, over time, with the practice of the awareness of *The 5-Fold Act of Divine Consciousness* and God's two aspects.

This enhanced awareness of how you are vibrating is an integral part of the practices and instruction that one learns in Nityananda Shaktipat Yoga. Change in Śiva's Māyā comes about by way of becoming more and more aware of how you are vibrating and taking more responsibility for this, your individual vibration. This is an important part of what we practice here.

All Must Retrace Their Path

The waters rise up from the sea as clouds,
Then fall as rain and run back into the sea
in streams; nothing can keep them from
returning to their source. Likewise, the soul
rising up from Thee cannot be kept from joining
Thee again, although it turns in many eddies on
its way back. A bird which rises up from the
earth and soars into the sky can find no place
to rest in mid air, but must return again to earth.
So indeed must all retrace their path, and when
the soul finds the way back to its source, it will
sink and be merged in Thee, Oh Arunachala,
Thou Ocean of Bliss!

Sri Ramana Maharshi

The path to God-realization is a path that you are destined to tread at some point in this life or future lifetimes. At some point in the evolution of your Kārmas, you will have nowhere else to turn and nowhere else to look but to God. You can make the commitment to make the journey to Liberation now, or you can put it off for another lifetime. However, it is inevitable that you will reach a point in a particular life of yours when you will have to retrace your path back to God.

All beings eventually seek out a Master who can show them the way back. You can choose to do it now or you can do it later. If you choose to do it now, a true Paradise of ultimate Freedom, Total Joy, Complete Happiness, All-encompassing Bliss and Total insulation from the "rat race" of pleasure and pain will be your steady experience, by the Grace of the Master and your practice. Why wait?

Faith

Gurudev Bhagawān Nityānanda's third essential teaching is faith in God. The following is an excerpt from *Bhagawān Nityānanda of Ganeshpuri* by Paramahamsa Muktānanda.

The Bhagavad Gita says,

shraddhāvānl labhate jñānam [4:39]

One who possesses faith attains knowledge.

The essence of faith is to believe the unseen is as real as the seen. Faith is the root of all dharmas, all religions. To have complete faith in the feet of the Lord is the first and foremost way of attaining devotion. Every day with faith we should sing the praises of God, contemplating His qualities, His acts, and His beautiful names. In this way, our devotion will become strong. By singing His attributes, they will permeate our minds. By contemplating Him and following Him, love will arise in our hearts, and we will cross the ocean of worldliness.

Faith creates amazing miracles. Faith makes the earth move; faith makes a weak person strong; faith makes possible the impossible. Faith does not argue or debate with anyone. Without faith, life is as dry as a dessert is without sweetness. Faith is the magnet to attract God's Grace. Faith is the root of victory. Faith attains the unattainable. Faith makes it possible to experience Nityānanda in the heart. Faith in God turns poison into nectar. Therefore, Shree Gurudev used to say, "Have faith, have faith!"

With faith, a person can cross any kind of difficulty. Without faith, he drowns in the ocean of worldliness. Living without faith is a form of death. The Bhagavad Gita says that lack of faith, cynicism, leads to an endless cycle of birth and death:

Ashraddadhānāh purusha dharmasyāya paramtapa /
aprāpya mām nivartante mrityusamsāravartmani // [9:3]

Those who have no faith in this knowledge, Arjuna, do not
attain Me and are born again on the path of death and
transmigration.

Therefore, have faith. You will be able to see the Guru manifesting in your own Self. It is faith that makes fruitful the mantra, the deity, and prasad. And on the same topic the Bhagavad Gita says, shraddhāmayo 'yam purusho [17:3]

Faith constitutes the very essence of a human being.

Muktānanda Parāmahamsa
Bhagawān Nityānanda of Ganeshpuri

DHĀRANĀS

This Entire Universe Exists Inside You

The 5-Fold Act of Divine Consciousness is a very profound Siddha Science that requires study under the guidance of a Shaiva Sadguru to understand. These principles are further elaborated, in-depth, in our Nityananda Shaktipat Yoga curriculum. However, you can begin to have your own experience of this 5-Fold Act inside yourself through the practice of *Dharana.*

The following are a sampling of contemplations designed to help you imbibe the deepest meaning of the Sūtras you have just read. We recommend you contemplate each separately. To contemplate means to steadily regard with your heart, without prejudging or forming premature notions about that which you are contemplating.

* * *

That in which all this creation is established and from whence it arises is nowhere obstructed because it is, by its very nature, beyond all that is limiting and it is unaffected by any limitation anywhere.

Spanda-Kārikās 2:1

* * *

Neither this world, nor a friend, nor a relative belongs to me at all. When you are all this who else then could be mine? You, O Master, are the Great Lord. You are in truth the entire world. Thus, asking for any one specific thing is just the asking and nothing more.

Supremacy over the three worlds appears as trifling as a piece of straw to those who are devoted to you. What other fruit than your remembrance need their good deeds bear? When nothing at all is different from you and even the creator of the worlds is your creation, there is no need then to sing the praises of your miraculous deeds.

Utpaladeva
Śivastotrāvalī

* * *

Superimposition is the apparent presentation to consciousness, by the memory, of something previously observed elsewhere.

Sri Śankaracarya
Viveka Chudāmani

We see a snake. We remember it. The next day, we see a coil of rope. We superimpose the memory of the snake on it and mistake its true nature as a result.

* * *

Contemplate the entire universe or your own body simultaneously in its totality, as filled with your (essential, spiritual) bliss. Then, through your own ambrosia-like bliss, you will become identified with Supreme Bliss.

* * *

If Consciousness did not recognize a mountain, would it exist as a mountain? Consciousness alone exists, Consciousness alone is all this, all this is filled with Consciousness. I, you and all this world, are but Consciousness.

Vāsistha
Yoga Vāsistha
The Story of Bali

* * *

This same infinite Self conceives within itself the duality of oneself and the other. The mind arises, as a wave arises when the surface of the calm ocean is disturbed. But, please bear in mind that just as a bracelet of gold is but gold (and though gold exists without being a bracelet, a bracelet cannot exist without gold or other metal), the qualities and the nature of the created, and the potentiality of creation, are inherent in the Creator. The mind is not different from and has no existence independent of the infinite Self.

Vāsiṣṭha
Yoga Vāsiṣṭha
The Section on Creation

* * *

The Inner Self is the stage on which this Universe unfolds.

Śiva Sūtras 3:10

* * *

The individual experient also, in whom chiti or consciousness is contracted has the universe as his body in a contracted form.

Pratyabhijñāhṛdayam 4

* * *

The luminous being, Śiva, who is the perfect I-consciousness, takes the form of Spanda Śakti that is inherent in the multitude of words. The essence of this Spanda is the knowledge of the highest non-dualism and is the secret of mantra.

Śiva Sūtras 2:3

* * *

Moreover, the powers of speech are always ready to obscure his nature, as no mental representation can arise unpenetrated by speech.

Spanda-Kārikās 3:15

* * *

There are no sounds, meanings or thoughts that are not Śiva. It is He who is the only enjoyer, abiding always and everywhere as the object of enjoyment.

Spanda-Kārikās 2:4

* * *

Find a quiet place to sit comfortably and close your eyes. Place your entire focus on your breathing by listening intently to the sound your breath makes as you inhale and exhale. Sit and listen to this sound with total concentration.

Now, you will notice that, after you breathe in, there is a slight pause in your breathing before you exhale. You will also notice that, after you exhale, there is another slight pause before you start to breathe in again. Now, focus your attention on this space between your in breath and your out breath. Keep your attention on these spaces for as long as you can.

* * *

Even in this condition (of the individual bound soul) he (the individual) does the five kṛtyas (deeds) like Him (Śiva).

Pratyabhijñāhṛdayam 10

* * *

One who has become a compact mass of delusion, due to attachment to pain and pleasure, is involved in good and evil deeds.

Śiva Sūtras 3:35

* * *

Being completely free from the influence of pleasure and pain, one is fully established in his real Self as sheer Consciousness.

Śiva Sūtras 3:34

* * *

The person who strives constantly to discern the Spanda principle (in everything and everyone, everywhere) rapidly attains his own (natural, free) state of being, even while in the waking state itself.

Spanda-Kārikās 1:21

* * *

Within your being is an energy that rises and falls on your breath. As you breathe in slowly and steadily, you will observe that there is a pause after you complete your in-breath, before you begin breathing out. There is another natural pause after you slowly and steadily breathe out, before you begin to breathe in again. This is the space between your breaths. Keep your mind focused on these two spaces between the breaths, as you breathe in and breathe out slowly and steadily.

* * *

Right now, imagine a deep, black void of nothingness within yourself. You may visualize this void inside your being. Keep your mind fixed on this void. See what you are seeing. Feel what you're feeling. If your mind begins to wander from this void that you are visualizing, gently bring it back to focus on this void of nothing.

* * *

Right now, fix your mind on any point in front of you. Pick a place in space or on the wall or the floor. Do not pick a point on another person. Now, keep your mind fixed on this point by watching that point. See what you are seeing. Feel what you are feeling. If your mind begins to wander from the point you are looking at, gently bring it back to focus on this point and remove all thoughts from your mind.

* * *

Contemplate a void. It may help you to visualize a deep, black space of nothing. Focus on the spaces between your thoughts as you empty your mind of all thought. Now softly utter the syllable "Ah" and contemplate that syllable dissolving in that same void. Now contemplate that same void and allow the syllable "Ah" to rise out of that void and then subside back into it.

* * *

Contemplate that your body is without any support whatsoever. Imagine with firm belief that there is nothing below you to support you and nothing above you either. You are balanced in a void of nothing. You are just there with no support. Contemplate this now.

* * *

Contemplate a bright, blue endless sky, just like you have seen it before. See this sky now in your mind's eye...so vast and endless. Imagine this bright blue sky to be the very essence of God. Now contemplate this blue sky dissolving into your head. Imagine that this sky is entering your head now and dissolving there. See it dissolve there.

Nityananda Shaktipat Yoga
With Supreme Love and Devotion
We Welcome You With Our One Heart

Many people who have attended weekly programs and Sadguru Kedarji's weekend Shaktipat Blessing retreats have openly expressed the experiences they have had and continue to have as a result of following him and the methods and practices he instructs. We invite you to read some of these experience shares for yourself by logging on to

https://www.nityanandashaktipatyoga.org/programs-courses-events/experience-shares/

For more information about Kedarji's instruction and where to attend a Nityananda Shaktipat Meditation program log on to NityanandaShaktipatYoga.org, email us at info@nityanandashaktipatyoga.org or call our office at 330-623-7388, Ext 10.

Simple Pronunciation Table

Below we have selected common transliteration from Sanskrit vowels and consonants and given you an English word that will aide you in its proper pronunciation. Please see the glossary for further information.

a	as in cup.
ā	as in father.
i	as in fill or lily.
ī	as in seen.
u	as in full.
ū	as in rude.
ṛi	as in written.
ṛī	as in marine.
e	as in cave.
c	as in church.
ai	as in aisle.
o	as in stone.
au	as in house.
ś	as in sure.
ṣ	as in shun or bush
s	as in saint.
d	as in the th in gather.

GLOSSARY

The following is a glossary of sanskrit terms used in this book. Please refer to the pronunciation table on the previous page for the correct pronunciation of words and terms in this glossary.

Abhinavagupta
the great sage of The Spanda School and Trika Kashmir Shaivism. Abhinavagupta is credited with bringing Trika Shaivism and Spanda Yoga to the height of its philosophy and practice in the 10th century. He is the author of many treatises including *Tantrāloka* and *Parātriśikā Vivaraṇa*.

Ācārya
(acharya) great teacher; a Siddha, Siddhacharya or Guru; a perfected master of yoga.

Āgama
a scripture or sacred text.

Aghora
the purest Śakti of Śiva; one of the energies of Supreme Consciousness that is responsible for revealing God by taking the form of Mantra; the Goddess Maha Spanda.

Ahaṃkāras
the Ego; one of The City of Eight.

Ānanda
the Bliss of the Absolute; described as pure Joy; the essence of Divine Consciousness.

Anuttara
none higher; the Ultimate or Absolute beyond which there is nothing; the all-encompassing Supreme Being; all-pervasive God Consciousness.

Baba
an affectionate term given a Sadguru, literally means father.

Bade Baba
an affectionate name for Bhagawān Nityānanda of Ganeshpuri; Big Baba.

Bhagavad Gītā
the great song-sermon and sacred text in which Lord Krishna reveals to Arjuna the means to Liberation; a sacred text of Vedanta.

Bhagawān Nityānanda
the great modern sage of India who took up residence in Ganeshpuri until his passing in 1961; an Avatar who traveled the world in mysterious ways to heal the sick and free people from ignorance of the Truth; the Master of Sadguru Kedārji's lineage.

Bhakti
love and devotion for God and the Guru; surrender to God's Will.

Bindu
(also Vindu, Bindi) point; a representation of the transcendental and immanent aspects of Divine Consciousness; an expression of Śiva's Vimarśa aspect.

Buddhi
infinite intelligence; the will of God; the individual intellect; one of The City of Eight.

Chiti
(also Citi, Cit, Chit, Chiti Śakti) the Vimarśa (active) aspect of Śiva; Spanda Śakti; Śiva's independent, sovereign power.

Chiti Śakti
(see "Chiti" above)

Concealment
the fourth of the 5 deeds; the fourth of the 5-Fold Act of Divine Consciousness in which the Absolute conceals its true nature.

Dhāranā
a contemplation; a centering technique designed to make the mind quiet; the uninterrupted awareness of Śiva Consciousness.

Dharma

righteousness; essential duty; the act of loving Truth more than mundane life itself.

Divine Consciousness

Śiva Consciousness; the God-principle or Śiva-Śakti principle that exists in everything and everyone, everywhere; that which is uncreated and is responsible for the creation, sustenance and withdrawal of the entire universe; Anuttara.

Ghorā Śakti

(the terrible powers) the grouping of powers or phonemes that provide worldly pleasures to people and put obstacles in their path to spiritual progress.

God-principle

Divine Consciousness existing inside all sentient and insentient beings and everywhere else.

God-realization

liberation from ignorance of the Self; the goal of the Nityananda Shaktipat Yoga path; the state of constant rapture; the uninterrupted experience of Bliss, Joy, Inner Peace and Total Freedom that rises from permanent union with Śiva-Śakti; the permanent experience of seeing God in everything and everyone, everywhere.

Grace

the power that creates, sustains and withdraws this entire Universe; Anuttara; that which reveals God; the Divine Energy that is transmitted upon the receipt of Śaktipat from a Siddha; the power at work through a Siddha that guides and nurtures the student on the spiritual path; the Grace-bestowing power of God.

Guru

literally from darkness to light; a Siddha or Sadguru who leads you from the darkness of spiritual ignorance to the light of God; a spiritual leader who is a spiritually-perfected Love being and Master of Siddha Science.

Gurudev
an affectionate name for the Guru, or Master; a Siddha.

Iccā
Divine Will; the immanent aspect of Divine Will (individual will) at work in humankind; one of Śiva's divine powers.

Jāgrat
wakefulness; the waking state; one of the coverings concealing the true nature of the Self; one of the four bodies.

Jīva
the individual bound soul who is ignorant of the Truth that God exists everywhere, in everything and everyone.

Jīvanmukti
the state of a Jīvanmukta; liberation while still in the body; the permanent experience of merging with the Absolute while still in the body.

Jñāna
(also gyaana, pronounced "ynaana") knowledge of the Absolute borne of direct experience; divine knowledge that rises spontaneously from within.

Jñāneshwar Mahāraj
(pronounced "ynaaneshwar," also Jñāneshwar, Jñānadevā) the 13th century poet-saint and Siddha who established the Bhakti movement in Medieval times and was the leader of the Natha Sect. He is credited with making Śaktipat and spiritual practice accessible to the common people at a time when these practices were reserved only for those of the highest caste; the author of several sacred texts including *Jñāneshwari* and *Amṛitānubhav*.

Kārma
action that creates future consequences (either positive or negative) for one who believes he/she is the "doer;" the law of cause and effect; action that is tainted by the belief that one is the body with an ego that possesses; the reason you are born and die over and over again, purposeless activity.

Kārmaśaya
the pot of Kārmas that functions in the relative modes of time, space, cause and effect.

Kaulikī
the emissional power of God; Spanda; the power of manifestation of the Lord; Śakti.

Kaulinī
(see Kaulikī above)

Kriyā
one of Śiva's 3 powers representing the spontaneous vibration and activity of the Divine; activity or action perceived in the world of forms; spontaneous movements of Śakti inside one's being (often experienced during meditation and chanting or in the company of a Siddha) that result from the purifying activity of Kuṇḍalinī Śakti after the receipt of Śaktipat.

Kṛtyas
literally deeds; a reference to The 5-Fold Act of Divine Consciousness.

Kula
group or grouping of energies; sangham or spiritual community formed around a Siddha; of Śiva or pertaining to Śiva; the path of union with Śiva through the rising of Kuṇḍalinī Śakti into Sahasrar; the Siddha Path; the Wheel of Energies of Lord Śiva; Śiva Consciousness.

Kuṇḍalinī Śakti
(also Kuṇḍalinī) a specific aspect of Spanda (spiritual energy) that lies dormant at the base of the spine in three-and-a-half folds until awakened by a Siddha through Śaktipat; the inner energy responsible for purifying The City of Eight when nurtured by spiritual practice after Śaktipat; the inner energy that, upon the culmination of sadhana, merges with Śiva in the Sahasrar.

Mahā
the great; the highest; the Ultimate or Absolute.

Mahādev
most high; another name for Lord Śiva; another name for Lord Rudra.

Mahāghora Śakti
(literally "the most terrible") the group of energies responsible for keeping the ignorant bound to the cycle of birth and death; the Śaktis responsible for concealing God from those who are attached to worldly pleasures and sense pleasures.

Mahā Spanda
(also Chit or Chiti) the highest, purest form of spiritual energy or Śakti; Śiva's active aspect or emissional power; Visarga.

Madhyamā
the third stage of the manifestation of language; the level of subtle speech where letters begin to become fully formed through thought.

Manas
(also Chitta) the mind.

Manifestation
the first of the 5 deeds; the first of the 5-Fold Act of Divine Consciousness in which the Absolute manifests a world-appearance within the body of Supreme Consciousness.

Mātrikā Śakti
(also Mātrikā, Matṛka, Mātrukā) the power of sound inherent in the letters of the alphabet; the power of words that is the foundation for the manifestation of objects; the emissional power or Visarga of Lord Śiva that manifests the 50 phonemes or cognitions.

Māyā Śakti
(also Māyā or Śiva's Māyā) see "Śiva's Māyā" below.

Nimeṣa
literally "closing of the eye;" the withdrawal of the Universe back into the Absolute; the withdrawal of Chiti or Spanda Śakti back into Śiva when all perception/cognition is destroyed and all activity ceases.

Parā
the formless Śiva-Śakti principle in its state of undivided unity.

Parama Śiva
(also Parāmśiva) the Absolute, formless God; the Supreme Being.

Paśupati
another name for Lord Śiva; a reference to one of Śiva's powers used as a weapon to destroy evil and to also withdraw the Universe; a reference to Lord Rudra.

Paśyantī
the recognizable stir in Śiva Consciousness that is still undistinguishable; the second level of speech manifestation where sound and its source exist in undistinguishable unity; sound existing in seed form that is not yet manifest.

Prakāśa
Śiva's static or transcendental aspect in which Spanda exists in seed form; the light of Śiva Consciousness that gives power to light; the light of Divine Consciousness.

Prāṇa
the life force; the vital breath; the Vibration of Divine Consciousness that travels along the breath.

Prāṇa Śakti
the aspect of Spanda or Chiti that causes the breath to move in the body; the power that drives the breath; that which causes Kuṇḍalinī Śakti to rise inside the Suṣumnā Nādi.

Pratyabhijñāhṛdayam
(pronounced "pratya-bidge-ynaa-rid-dayam") the doctrine of Supreme Recognition; one of the Shaiva Āgamas and primary sacred texts of Trika Shaivism written by Kṣemarāja, the foremost disciple of Abhinavaguptacharya.

Pṛithvī
Earth; Earth Tattva.

Pure Perceiving Awareness
the Supreme awareness that exists at all times in one's own being and everywhere else, before thoughts, notions, and ideas are superimposed in the mind.

Śaivism
the spiritual paths devoted to the worship of Śiva; the scriptures, sacred texts and Tantras on the practices leading to union with Śiva-Śakti.

Śakti
Lord Śiva's emissional power (Visarga) or manifestational power; spiritual energy; Vibration of Divine Consciousness; Spanda or Chiti; Vimarśa; the active power of God.

Śaktipat
the spiritual awakening imparted by a Siddha; the awakening of Kundalini Śakti by a Siddha; the final state of Liberation from ignorance (parāśaktipata) that is bestowed by Śiva.

Samādhi
a state of pure bliss in which there are no thoughts in the mind whatsoever; the nirvikalpa state arrived at in meditation; the final state of Liberation in which the yogi experiences God in everything and everyone, everywhere.

Samsārin
one who is deluded by his/her own powers into believing that the world is merely a world of forms; the individual bound soul who believes that he/she is the body and the ego and the mind that possesses objects.

Saṅkalpa
the will; the power of intention by which Spanda Śakti is directed outward for the purpose of manifestation; the Divine Will of God; the individual will.

Śankara
another name for Lord Śiva.

Sat-Chit
Being-Awareness; infinity; the state of the formless Absolute; beyond existence.

Siddha
(also Siddha Guru, Siddhāchārya, Siddhācārya) a perfected master of yoga who has attained, through spiritual practice, the highest state and become one with the Absolute, one with God; one who has reached the goal of all spiritual practice by merging (surrendering) the limitation of the ego (one's sense of individuality) into Śiva-Śakti, into the Supreme Consciousness of God, a Shaktipat Sadguru.

Siddha Lineage
the line of perfected masters of yoga or Sadgurus who have received Śaktipat and realized the goal of their spiritual practice through the instruction of their Masters; the unbroken path of Kaula teachings in Siddha Maha Yoga and Trika Śaivism that have passed on from Guru to Disciple since the Primordial Guru, Śiva, first taught disciples.

Śiva
(also Śiva, Lord Śiva, Lord Śiva) the Absolute; Divine Consciousness; the Supreme or Perfect "I" Consciousness of God; Brahman; the highest God-principle; the Guru principle; the Primordial Guru or Being; The Blue Being; Nileshwara.

Śiva Consciousness
the outlook of Śiva; Pure Perceiving Awareness; the vision of God everywhere and in everything; the experience that the universe does not exist but that only God exists; the act of seeing God in everything and everyone, everywhere.

Śiva's Māyā
(also Māyā, Māyā Śakti) that power that Śiva uses to survey himself; that which we refer to as the universe; this world-appearance that we call world; the appearance of a world and a universe where there is actually only Śiva and his Spanda Śakti; illusion; the illusion of a world.

Śiva-Śakti Principle
the God-principle that creates, sustains and withdraws the entire universe; that which is uncreated and changeless by its very nature; the cause of all things created and uncreated in this universe; the Supreme I-Consciousness of God; Sat-Chit Ānanda.

Spanda
(also Spanda Śakti) Universal Creative Vibration; Vibration of Divine Consciousness or the ceaseless pulse of Divine Consciousness; the slight or subtle movement of Divine Consciousness that is the foundation for the gross movement of the elements inside and out; the Wheel of Energies that ceaselessly creates, sustains and withdraws (recycles) this entire universe; one's own inner essence; that which creates the perception of a world where there is only Śiva; Śiva's emissional power or Visarga.

Spanda Yoga
(also the Spanda School, the Trika School, Trika Śaivism or Kashmir Shaivism) the Yoga science in which one undertakes the study of the union with and identification with Śiva through the steady experience of his Vimarśa aspect, Spanda or Chiti Śakti; the Siddha path to obtain union with your Natural, Free State of Being, without difficulty; a Raj Yoga that includes Śaktipat Diksha and the culmination of all other yogic practices.

Spanda-Kārikās
the stanzas on the Vibration of Divine Consciousness; a primary sacred text of Spanda Yoga and Trika Śaivism with important commentary and experience shares of the Saints and Siddhas of The Spanda School and the Siddha Lineage including Vasagupta, Kṣemarāja, Kallaṭabhaṭṭa, Rājānaka Rama and Bhagavadutapala.

Śri
great; holy; esteemed.

Superimposition
the projection into the body of Supreme Consciousness, from the memory, of something or someone previously experienced elsewhere.

Supreme Being
Anuttara; the Absolute; the Universal Being or God-principle; Lord Śiva.

Supreme Consciousness
(also Supreme Principle, Supreme Reality, the Ultimate) Chiti or Spanda Śakti; the independent Divine energy of Consciousness that manifests the entire Universe; Visarga; Śiva Consciousness.

Supreme Subject
Anuttara; the Absolute; the Śiva-Śakti principle; Lord Śiva.

Sustenance
the second of the 5-Fold Act of Divine Consciousness; Lord Śiva's act of sustaining the appearance of a world and a Universe.

Suṣumnā Nādi
(also Sushumna) the subtle body in which is contained the individual will or intellect, the ego, the mind, the five senses and their offspring; the City of Eight; the psychic apparatus known as Antaḥkaraṇa; the path that Kuṇḍalinī Śakti travels along as she rises to union with Śiva in the Sahasrār.

Sūtra
literally "to thread through;" an underlying principle that threads through all the rest, unifying a teaching or instruction with its Divine Source; a sacred principle that removes ignorance of the Self; Śiva-Śakti in the form of spiritual instruction.

Svapna
dreaming; the dream state; the world of your inner impressions; the second of the four bodies or coverings.

Swami
the title given to a monk, sannyasin, ascetic or God-realized being.

Swami Lakshmanjoo
the great saint of Kashmir who revived the doctrines and teachings of Trika Śaivism in the 20th Century.

Paramahamsa Muktānada
the great saint and Siddha Master who gave Śaktipat to Sadguru Kedārji and set him on the Siddha Path of Bhagawān Nityānanda.

Tattvas
the 36 primary levels or stages of manifestation of the universe and this world-appearance from Śiva down to this earth; the planes of existence that are all expressions of Śiva through his Spanda Śakti; the various forms of the Goddess Spanda.

The City of Eight
see Suṣumnā Nādi above.

The 5-Fold Act of Divine Consciousness
(also The 5 Kṛtyas or deeds, The 5-fold Act, The 5-Fold Act of God) the acts of Manifestation, Sustenance, Withdrawal, Concealment and Grace that are performed by God and also performed by the individual bound soul on a daily basis; the transcendental and immanent aspects of Śiva-Śakti.

The Wheel of Energies
the collective whole of Śaktis that can be experienced in the world of forms created by Chiti; the combined aspects of Spanda Śakti that create, sustain and withdraw the entire universe; Visarga.

Trika
meaning three; a reference to the divine God-principle of Śiva-Śakti-Nara (the absolute, his active aspect and the individual bound soul); a reference to the Advaita (non-dualistic) branch of Śaivism; also a reference to three of Śiva's powers, Icchā (divine will), Jñāna (divine knowledge), and Kriyā (purposeless action).

Turiya
(also Turya) the fourth body of a human being; the state of Meditation or Nirvikalpa state when all thoughts have ceased; a state of union with God.

Turyātīta
the state beyond the fourth; the super conscious state of Śivo'ham or Purnaham Vimarśa in which the yogi experiences complete Liberation from the bondage of ignorance ; the uninterrupted state of rapture that is the final union with Śiva; Śiva Drishti.

Unmeṣa
the creative expansion or manifestation of the Universe due to Śiva's independent Śakti; what you experience as you move from one thought or emotion to another; Visarga.

Vaikharī
one of the four levels or manifestations of sound as speech; the gross level of speech.

Vimarśa
(also Vimarśa Śakti) Śiva's active aspect; the emissional power of Supreme Consciousness; Spanda; Chiti; that which creates the perception of activity and objects.

Visarga
the emissional or manifestational power of the Absolute; that which creates, sustains and withdraws the entire Cosmos; bindu; the two points, representing the transcendental and immanent aspects of God, between which Śakti moves back and forth.

Viṣṇu
a reincarnation or manifestation of Lord Śiva; one who enjoys equal status with Śiva; the sustainer of the Universe.

Withdrawal
the third of the 5-Fold Act of Divine Consciousness when the Universe is withdrawn back into the formless Absolute; what occurs when the mind becomes silent and, with spiritual practice, dissolves.

Yuga
age; one of the ages in a world-cycle; a reference to the four Yugas that comprise one world cycle after which the entire Universe is withdrawn into Anuttara for a time before another world-cycle begins; Satya Yuga (the first or golden age), Treta Yuga (the second or silver age), Dvāpara Yuga (the third or bronze age), Kālī Yuga (the fourth or iron age).

INDEX

The Verses On Surrender

(the references 'we,' 'our' and 'us' are references to lovers of God who embrace the Guru)

1. Surrender is not handing over our free will to someone or something else. Surrender is the act of engaging our will, to align ourselves with God, so that we can experience our oneness with God. Our ego personality is a block that keeps us from experiencing our God-nature and God-power. So, we must Surrender the notion that we are the body, this ego personality, that we are small, powerless, finite beings, that we are impure. Surrender is embracing the Truth that we are one with God. It is the act of gaining the experience of this Cosmic Truth through the destruction of the ego idea.

2. If it is our goal to know and merge in God, how can we ever hope to do it if we do not have someone who has already done it showing us the way? We need someone who is the very personification of That Supreme Self. We have to Surrender to the one who is the full embodiment of the knowledge of the highest, in order to experience that knowledge for ourselves.

3. Some people believe that surrendering to a Siddha Guru means that they are Surrendering to just a person. However, when you Surrender to a Siddha, you are Surrendering to both God and the Will of God. A living Siddha Guru is not just a person, as neither are you. A Siddha Guru is the full embodiment of the Guru-principle whose individual identity has been erased by his Guru. This makes such a being a perfect conduit for God's power of Grace. It is reflected in the state of Liberation that sets a perfect example of leadership, as well as a model for the state to be attained in the moment, from moment-to-moment. Therefore, test the Guru first.

4. To destroy the limitation of the ego, we need a bond of power, a perfect relationship with a being who has fully imbibed that God-power. A Shaktipat Siddha Guru is such a being. Surrendering to a Siddha is different than Surrendering to any other. Why? Because a Siddha is a being who no longer has an individual will. A Siddha is one who lives in the highest experience of God, an experience higher than angelic and heavenly beings have, or even the Gods themselves have.

5. This highest experience of God is a state of ego-less-ness and a state where the Siddha has merged his individual identity and will entirely in

God. This means that a Siddha is a God-Realized being, a catalyst, and a pure untainted vessel for God's Will, Power and Grace. Such beings can only give Grace, even if that appears to be imparted casually. So, when we Surrender to a Siddha we Surrender to the Absolute, the One God that is our God-nature. We are surrendering to our own inner Self.

6. We Surrender to our highest Self, to Grace, to what Sadguru Kedarji calls the Guru-principle that is at work through the Guru. Without this Surrender, Liberation from our own ignorance is not possible. The Guru has practiced and perfected Surrender and now lives in a state of complete, perfect Surrender to the same Divine Guru-Principle, reflected in his own constant inner worship of his own Guru.

7. A Siddha Guru is a perfected disciple, remaining a disciple of his own Guru, even after his Guru's passing from this plane. Therefore, the only difference between you and a Siddha Guru is that such a being has become established in the perfection of Discipleship, while you are still making the journey to that perfection.

8. Knowing what to Surrender is vital. We surrender the limitation of our egos and the restless mind and with that, we gain Grace and attain the Lord Himself. We have to Surrender our thoughts and notions. To Surrender is to have a quiet mind that is no longer restless and embraces silence.

9. Surrender is eliminating or giving up the notions of ego personality and all associated limitations. Surrender is the act of firmly placing attention on the Supreme "I" Consciousness, to merge in that Source until we lose our individual identity in that Ultimate Reality. In order to do this, we must release all association with our being just the mind, the body and the senses – just a person.

10. Surrender is an absolute necessity in order to break attachments, limiting desires/cravings and other false notions and tendencies. Surrender is also the dedication of body, mind and all action to the glorification of God. It is performing our spiritual practices as instructed by our Guru. We must Surrender all actions to God.

11. Make everything a blessed sacrament to the Lord and, in time, we will be released from egoism because we will have practiced Surrendering the

notion of doership. By practicing this one principle alone we embrace our oneness with God, our oneness with the Guru, and are able to Surrender to this Truth. This is how Bhakti, Devotion, is best cultivated.

12. This Surrender is a matter of letting go of the desire to possess, acquire and appropriate people, places and things to ourselves. We need to Surrender the notion of being the one who does things, who makes things happen. We need to let go of any false sense of control that we have.

13. Sadguru Kedarji says that desire cannot quench desire. The satisfaction or content experienced in Surrender comes from the absence of limiting desire and craving. Surrender is a state of Grace in which there is the experience of being satisfied with whatever God gives us without wanting to add or take anything away from what we are given.

THY WILL BE DONE, THY WILL BE DONE, THY WILL BE DONE.

14. We also need to Surrender our wrong, useless understandings and our habitual, useless thinking by submitting to the most useful understandings that the Guru imparts. Even though things appear a certain way to us, this does not always mean that the way they appear is the truth, or even real. After all, until the final dawning of Liberation, we filter everything through the limitation of the ego that is a perceiving mechanism tainted by our mental conditioning, our karmas.

15. So, with Faith, we need to remain open to the possibility that how things appear to us in the moment may be tainted by how each of us filters our experience of people, places and things through the play of the impurities – the Gunas and the Malas. This is a good way to begin practicing Surrender by imbibing the right understanding imparted by the Guru and our Siddha lineage. Because if we do just that much, we open ourselves up to Grace and experience a new, greater benefit. If we don't open ourselves up to this new direction, how will we ever know and experience a shift in our awareness? How will we ever experience the ocean of Grace that comes with a heightened witnessing awareness?

16. We can start small and continue to increase our Faith and Surrender as we gain the proof our restless mind seeks. If ever our Faith waivers from what the right understanding is, it is our duty to ask our Guru or pray to God inwardly, right away in that moment, before resisting Surrender. For

transformation can only happen in the present moment.

17. As we practice Surrender to the Truth, to our God-nature, the quality of our surrender is tested. Due to our ego attachments, it is easy to resist the Truth and we may even decide not to Surrender at all. Egoism is very ingrained in us. We have lifetimes of past impressions and pre-dispositions that we carry around with us. It is easy to do what we have always done and to defend the ego that is the storehouse of all of our beliefs, notions and useless understandings.

18. It is understandable why the limitation of the ego does not want to take a risk in leaving off what it knows, at first. The ego idea is not acclimated to serving the Self. So, we have to surrender the ego entirely, so that it meets with its own destruction. If we don't let it go, we will never experience what lies beyond the limited experience of life that we have come to know. How can we ever grow and develop spiritually if we are not willing to set aside what we think we know, or what we think we believe in, in order to experience what is evident when we do Surrender?

19. At times, we allow the limitation of the ego to behave like a feral animal. A wild animal operates in a defensive, survival mode when faced with a new experience that it perceives as uncomfortable or dangerous. However, we are not feral animals. We have taken a human birth that allows for the experience of a heightened spiritual witnessing awareness, rather than a fear-based reaction.

20. How can we ever hope to know God, how can we even call ourselves human beings, if we act like wild animals, guarding our egoism?

21. Surrender is abandoning fear, abandoning what we think we know, abandoning what we are attached to, in favor of the Self. Even a little bit of Faith can go a long way in helping us to Surrender to the Truth of our God-nature.

22. The necessary effort for practicing Surrender is different for each of us because we each have different karmas, along with varying levels of attachment and aversion. So, whatever tests and instruction we are given, these are tailored made for us by God, embodied in the form of the living Master; So that we can rise above our deep attachments to a world of fantasy; So that we can easily experience God in everything and everyone,

everywhere.

23. We engage in the discipline of Surrender in order to discard limitations that stand in the way of our experience of God. All of the instruction and practices we are offered in Nityananda Shaktipat Yoga – these are tools for our use to discard limitation and tap into an ego-less state where we can experience what Surrender and this Natural Free State of Being actually is.

24. It is certain that, when we find ourselves experiencing resistance to Surrender, our mind is not absorbed in God or the instruction of the Guru. The only time we will ever find it difficult to Surrender is when we maintain our egotistical outlook, holding on to unfounded beliefs because we are not actively performing our Sadhana with vigilance.

25. Only an undisciplined person who is not applying the instruction given lacks Surrender. If we lack Surrender, we can be sure that we are fighting with the spiritual generosity, the Grace of the Guru and God. We are then taking for granted the blessing of Grace we are being given to rise above limitation and contraction to experience our God-nature, our God-power. For this reason, we should avoid clinging to limiting desire and craving and our worldly fantasies.

26. Therefore, if we want Liberation, it is our duty to Surrender completely. There is no other way. So, we must decide which we want. Do we want to continue living the same limited existence filtered through the perceptions of the limitation of the ego? Or, do we want to Surrender and merge in the Truth? For, there is not enough room for both. We have to choose one or the other.

27. When we Surrender to a Sadguru (true spiritual leader with the power to transmit Grace), we need to do so with the proper understanding of how the relationship works. It goes like this. A Siddha Guru instructs and the aspiring disciple obeys. We each have to decide if we are willing and prepared to undergo any test, to follow any degree of necessary discipline, to do what it takes to experience, know and merge with God.

28. That means that we do not get to choose what kind of tests we will undergo. We simply Surrender to whatever comes. We shouldn't attempt to alter the discipline being taught to free us in order to please the very

ego that we seek to Surrender! Once we decide that we want all-consuming Love for God, along with the Grace necessary to reside in that state, then we have to let go with full Faith, relying on our growing experience of the Self, knowing that God will protect and bless us when we Surrender to Him.

29. Until perfected, Surrender is always a practice. No one gets it right all at once.

30. As we practice Surrender as instructed, we have to continually discard any false understandings about someone making us do something that we do not want to do. This understanding is one that many people embrace about Surrender and it holds them back. It is not even the Truth. A Siddha Guru will never force us to do anything. With a Siddha we always have the choice to decide if we want the limitation of the ego, cloaked in our false identity as just a person, or if we want the Truth.

31. When we Surrender we are letting go of the false identification with being just the mind, just the body and the senses. We are also embracing the discipline necessary for releasing our attachment to people, places and things, along with our limiting desires and cravings. This is very important to remember, especially in those moments when the ego resists what is necessary for us to engage in order to practice Surrender.

32. It is only after Surrendering that we experience the benefit of egolessness. In other words, you cannot know the benefit of Surrender until you've employed the methods for testing and practicing it in the laboratory of your own existence, over an extended period of time. Some degree of Trust and Faith must be engaged first before we can experience the benefit of Surrender. There is no other way.

33. Slowly we gain the Faith to Surrender and endure any test necessary. We gain this Faith through our Devotion to God, our Devotion to the living Sadguru and the review of our growing experiences under the Sadguru's leadership to confirm that we are not engaged in blind faith.

34. We cannot fully imbibe God's Grace without Surrender of the ego. When we Surrender completely by the methods, instruction and Grace of the Guru, the Surrender itself is effortless. Then there is an inspired, spontaneous outpouring of Grace that moves our witnessing awareness

into the heart of the Supreme.

35. To Surrender is to switch the tracks of the train you are on, changing your destination in Consciousness from that of worldly bondage to merge in God-Consciousness.

36. It takes Trust, Faith, Devotion, Patience, Humility, Reverence, Longing and Love to Surrender the limitation of the ego. These spiritual principles are easily cultivated over time by keeping the company of a Siddha Guru and obeying his instruction.

37. Surrender is Love. The two cannot be separated.

38. We are always practicing at Surrender until we merge in it. In this way, Surrender is the embodiment of egolessness.

39. The tests that we undergo are to show us our ego and to serve as the proof of our Surrender or lack of it. After a test, a person knows how complete or lacking his/her attainment in Surrender is. In full Surrender, regardless of the test, it is effortless.

40. Sadguru Kedarji's leadership includes instruction in time-honored methods for cultivating patience, while discarding limiting desire and craving. One who claims to Surrender the ego but gets upset when it comes time to do so, is not recognizing the power of Grace inherent in Surrender. This makes it more difficult to let go of the ego-idea.

41. How then can Grace ever release you from the suffering wrought by attachment? If you are willfully upset for not getting your way, you are not embracing the steps to aligning yourself with God's Will.

42. So, Surrender is also the act of keeping our attention focused on God and the Guru. If our attention is scattered in various, worldly directions, it will be impossible to perfect Surrender.

43. True Surrender is to do whatever our chosen Guru tells us to do, without question, without hesitation and with a happy heart. Only a Siddha Guru knows what limitations and attachments must be broken in order for us to experience God as our very own Self.

44. The practice of Surrender is the privilege to receive Blessings that attract Grace. It is following the Guru's command without any conditions. It is obeying our chosen Master's every instruction and offering implicit reverence with full remembrance that we are Surrendering to the Shakti, the Will of God reflected in the Guru. Therefore, test the Guru first.

45. We need to maintain the awareness that we are Surrendering to the Divine Shakti, our very own Self. In doing so, over time, we will have the experience of merging in God's Will.

46. What should we do if we experience disharmony because of an inner conflict, a resistance to Surrender? One example is to do as couples do in a marriage.

47. An example is this: If there is a conflict in a marriage, the couple must discard or Surrender opposition, whatever the couple is disagreeing on, in favor of the commitment to the marriage. As long as the couple's commitment to remain in the marriage is greater than their disagreement, sacrifices are then made in favor of harmony.

48. With the Guru it's the same premise but with one big difference. We shouldn't attempt to negotiate with the Guru as one would barter needs for wants in other relationships or a business deal. We have to make the decision to follow the Guru implicitly, in favor of our commitment to Liberation.

49. A true Guru will never make any attempt to force us into that decision. The choice is always with us, in every moment. But we do have to keep making the decision to let go in order to go higher in our spiritual evolution. After all, Liberation, reflected in the state of the Sadguru, is so splendid that it cannot bear the cheap price tag of egoism.

50. When we Surrender, we allow God's Grace to penetrate us and, in doing so, we become one with our God-nature and God-power. Surrender is Jñana, true knowledge and, in its fullness, is the state of Liberation.

51. You may have had your own experiences of the benefit, the usefulness of Surrender of the ego. Remembering that experience serves as a constant reminder of the value of making this state of Surrender a permanent state.

52. Surrender is letting go of attachment to everything and everyone. In this way, true Surrender is Liberation. Liberation is not some foreign attainment separate from you. Liberation is innate within each of us. We can practice and experience Liberation, moment by moment, by perfecting our Surrender. Once we finally let go of everything, knowing that there is nothing for us to gain or lose, in that moment we experience what it is to be Liberated. In that moment the ego personality dies and we are transformed beyond dimension and time. We can then burst with the sweet nectar of the Self.

53. When we Surrender we open ourselves to the Ultimate Reality and that Cosmic force pours into us. We transcend the limitation of individuality and merge with all of existence. We are no longer separate, we are no longer finite. We become united and indistinguishable from the Absolute.

54. Surrender is giving up the idea of a body, transcending separateness and duality by exploding out of our little cocoon, shattering the shell of our limited ego idea and expanding outward in all directions, across all dimensions - until we are merged with every particle in the Universe and master all the energies of our lives. When we Surrender, we allow God's Grace to penetrate us and, in doing so, we become one with God.

55. In truth, Surrender is an educational term used for the benefit of those still imprisoned in the ego-idea. To one who has Surrendered all attachments and aversions, there is only indescribable Joy in which even the notion of Surrender no longer exists.

56. Surrender of the ego is an absolute necessity in order to break attachments, limiting desire and craving, and the false notion of individuality. Surrender is also the dedication of body, mind, senses and all action to the glorification of God. It is performing our spiritual practice with vigilance, as instructed by the Guru.

57. We must Surrender all actions to God. Make everything a blessed sacrament and, in time, we will be released of egoism because we will have practiced Surrendering the notion of doership. By practicing this one principle alone we enforce our oneness with God, our oneness with the Guru, and are able to Surrender to this Truth. This is how Bhakti, Devotion, is best cultivated.

58. Your independence of will and judgment alone, cause you to stand upright like God. Therefore, Surrender is not handing over your free will to someone or something else. Surrender is the act of choosing to engage your will, to align yourself with God's Will, so that you can experience your oneness with God.

59. The easy means for doing so is to exercise your free will and judgment in testing the leadership and methods you are instructed in by the living Master, in the laboratory of your own existence, to prove the value of that leadership and instruction. In this way, the ego is Surrendered based on the proof of experience in the comparison of your state when you do Surrender versus when you don't. This risk/ratio test is the check to blind faith and the foundation for complete trust in the Guru's leadership, instruction and commands.

60. The limitation of the ego is a block that keeps us from experiencing God. So, we must Surrender the notions that we are the body/mind/senses, the ego idea, that we are small, powerless, finite beings, that we are impure. Surrender is embracing the Truth that we are one with God. It is also the act of gaining the experience of this Truth.

61. If it is our goal to know the Self and to merge in That, how can we ever hope to attain it if we do not have someone who has already attained that state to lead us? We need someone who is the very personification of God to lead the way. The easy means to practicing and imbibing Surrender is to Surrender to that one whose ego has been destroyed in the fire of his own Guru's Love.

62. Therefore, Surrender all that you are not, in the direct experience of your God-nature.

Ingram Content Group UK Ltd.
Milton Keynes UK
UKHW020730060623
422954UK00015B/840

9 798218 199159